Teaching Math
With Favorite Picture Books

Hands-on Activities and Reproducibles to Teach
Math Using More Than 25 Picture Books

By Judi Hechtman and Deborah Ellermeyer
with Sandra Ford Grove

SCHOLASTIC
PROFESSIONAL BOOKS

NEW YORK • TORONTO • LONDON • AUCKLAND • SYDNEY
MEXICO CITY • NEW DELHI • HONG KONG

To my special friend, Jerry Pallotta, who inspired me to write books
—Judi Hechtman

To my children, Anna and Jimmy
—Debbie Ellermeyer

To my mom and dad, Cathy and Horace, with love
—Sandra Ford Grove

Edited by Jean Liccione
Front cover and interior design by Kathy Massaro
Cover photographs by Donnelly Marks
Interior illustrations by Kate Flanagan
except pages 8, 32, 64 (menorah) and 69 by James Graham Hale

ISBN: 0-590-76250-8

Contents

Introduction

*W*elcome to *Teaching Math With Favorite Picture Books*. On the pages that follow, you'll find a wealth of ideas for using well-loved picture books to introduce math problems for children to explore. The book is filled with activities and reproducible patterns and recording sheets that combine problem-solving strategies with the introduction and reinforcement of math skills and concepts. Whether they're doing "donut addition" with *Imogene's Antlers*, patterning with *Caps for Sale*, or estimating and measuring with *Inch by Inch*, the activities will engage children in concrete mathematical experiences. They will enable you to teach mathematical concepts and skills, assess children's progress within authentic contexts, and extend mathematics to other areas of the curriculum.

What's Inside

Each activity in this book takes you from preparation to extensions. Here's an overview of what you'll find:

- suggestions for introducing the literature selection to students
- a list of the NCTM Standard(s) the activity supports
- a complete list of all materials necessary for the activity
- step-by-step directions, teaching tips, and grouping suggestions for doing the activity with your class
- ready-to-use reproducible recording sheets and patterns
- Across the Curriculum extensions that link the literature selection to other areas of your curriculum such as social studies, language arts, and art.

About the Literature Selections

We've chosen some books in which mathematics is the focus, others that have fairly obvious mathematical connections, and still others that are fun and fanciful stories—to demonstrate how math activities can grow from just about any book. So read on ... and see what new ideas you'll discover as you share literature with your class!

Teaching With the Standards

The National Council of Teachers of Mathematics (NCTM) has outlined 13 content standards that have become the basis for change in the way mathematics is taught and in how children are learning mathematics. Use the chart on the following page to see at a glance how each literature selection and its accompanying activities correlate with the Standards. Note that for each selection, the activities always represent the first four Standards: *Problem Solving*, *Communication*, *Reasoning*, and making *Connections* between math and children's lives.

Connections With the NCTM Standards

Title	Mathematics as Problem Solving	Mathematics as Communication	Mathematics as Reasoning	Mathematical Connections	Estimation	Number Sense and Numeration	Concepts of Whole Number Operations	Whole Number Computation	Geometry and Spatial Sense	Measurement	Statistics and Probability	Fractions and Decimals	Patterns and Relationships
Draw Me a Star	✽	✽	✽	✽		✽			✽				
Blast Off! A Space Counting Book	✽	✽	✽	✽		✽					✽		
Ten Black Dots	✽	✽	✽	✽			✽		✽				
"Band-Aids"	✽	✽	✽	✽			✽						
The King's Commissioners	✽	✽	✽	✽			✽	✽					
Math Curse	✽	✽	✽	✽				✽			✽		
The Crayon Counting Book	✽	✽	✽	✽		✽							✽
Imogene's Antlers	✽	✽	✽	✽			✽	✽	✽				
Domino Addition	✽	✽	✽	✽			✽	✽	✽				
The Quilt Story	✽	✽	✽	✽						✽			✽
The Greedy Triangle	✽	✽	✽	✽						✽			
Look at Annette	✽	✽	✽	✽						✽			✽
The Tangram Magician	✽	✽	✽	✽						✽			✽
Inch by Inch	✽	✽	✽	✽	✽					✽			
The Grouchy Ladybug	✽	✽	✽	✽						✽			✽
Alexander, Who Used to Be Rich Last Sunday	✽	✽	✽	✽				✽		✽	✽	✽	
A Chair for My Mother	✽	✽	✽	✽					✽	✽	✽		
Pigs Will Be Pigs	✽	✽	✽	✽			✽	✽		✽			
Time to…	✽	✽	✽	✽						✽		✽	✽
The M&M's® Brand Chocolate Candies Counting Book	✽	✽	✽	✽		✽	✽	✽			✽		
A Three Hat Day	✽	✽	✽	✽							✽		✽
Hanukkah!	✽	✽	✽	✽							✽		
Ed Emberley's Picture Pie	✽	✽	✽	✽						✽		✽	
Billy's Button	✽	✽	✽	✽									✽
Caps for Sale	✽	✽	✽	✽									✽
Jump, Frog, Jump	✽	✽	✽	✽									✽
The Important Book	✽	✽	✽	✽						✽			✽
Jesse Bear, What Will You Wear?	✽	✽	✽	✽							✽		✽

Draw Me a Star

BY ERIC CARLE • *Philomel, 1992*

INTRODUCING THE BOOK

Eric Carle's book begins as an artist draws a star, which inspires the creation of an entire universe. Show children the stars on the front and back covers of the book and ask them to compare and contrast them. Then read the story aloud, including the charming note from Eric Carle that explains his inspiration for writing the book. Invite children to demonstrate how they draw stars.

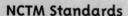

NCTM Standards

Estimation

Number Sense and Numeration

Counting Stars

Materials

🌀 timer or clock with a second hand

🌀 paper and pencil

1 Ask one child to draw a five-pointed star on the chalkboard. Then ask the child to draw another, this time stopping after each line is drawn. Other members of the class can follow along, "drawing" similar stars by moving their fingers in the air.

2 Next ask children to estimate how many five-pointed stars they think they can draw within a one-minute period of time. Share strategies for making estimates. For example, children could multiply the number of stars they can draw in 10 seconds by 6, or they could use repeated addition. Once children have an estimate, provide paper and pencils and invite children to test their estimates as you time them for one minute. Then have children count the number of stars they made and compare the actual number drawn to their original estimates.

3 Invite children to share what they learned about making estimates. Also ask them to explain their methods for counting their stars and keeping track of the number they counted.

Drawing Stars

Materials (for each child)

paper and pencil

1 Show children the drawing of the star on the back cover of Eric Carle's *Draw Me a Star*. Ask them to count the number of triangles contained within the star. Then refer back to Carle's step-by-step drawing of the star in the book. Have children practice drawing this eight-pointed star.

2 Encourage children to explore other ways to draw stars. With each star that is drawn, have them notice the inside shape and count the number of triangles made. Guide children to recognize the relationship between the number of triangles and the number of points on the star. Also discuss similarities and differences among the stars children draw.

Across the Curriculum

A SKY FULL OF STARS Examine with children the illustrations in *Draw Me a Star* and other books by Eric Carle. Help them note Carle's artistic style of layering and painting different colors of tissue paper to achieve various colors and effects. Have each child draw a large star from posterboard and cover it with tissue paper using Carle's layering and painting technique. Give your classroom a colorful, starry sky by hanging children's creations from the ceiling with string or yarn.

CLASSROOM STARS! Stars are often given a positive connotation: famous people are called stars; children often earn stars for good work. Have each child randomly select a classmate's name. Explain that they will create a star with that person's name on it and then write a statement telling something special about the person which makes him or her a class star. Some examples might be, "Stevie is our star artist" or "Mara is our star storyteller."

Blast Off!

A Space Counting Book

BY NORMA COLE • *Charlesbridge, 1994*

INTRODUCING THE BOOK

This book offers children the opportunity to count from 1 to 20, count by tens to 100, and to see much larger numbers in print as they learn facts about space and space travel. First read the top portion of each page aloud. As you read the book a second time, concentrate on the text in the bar at the bottom of each page. Have children raise their hands each time they hear a number mentioned during this reading.

NCTM Standards

Estimation

Statistics and Probability

ACTIVITY

Estimating Large Numbers

Materials (for each child)

- 8- by 8-inch construction paper square
- 2-inch construction paper frames (see below)
- paper and pencil

Ahead of Time

Prepare the construction paper squares and the frames. To make the 2-inch frames, fold 3- by 3-inch construction paper squares in half as shown and cut out a window, leaving a frame that is one inch wide. The inside dimensions should be 2 by 2 inches.

1 Return to the page in the book that focuses on counting to a trillion. Ask children if they think it would be possible to count every star in the sky. Discuss why this might be difficult, and ask children for ideas as to how it might be accomplished.

2 Give each child an 8- by 8-inch square of construction paper. Ask children to randomly fill their squares with drawings of stars of different sizes. Once this task is completed, instruct them to fold their square in half and then in half again into quarters. Demonstrate to children how to repeat the folding another time, and then unfold the paper, creating 16 square boxes within the 8- by 8-inch square.

3 Give children each a 2-inch frame and have them drop it randomly four times onto their star paper. After each drop they should count the number of whole stars inside the frame and record the count. Ask children to look at the four counts. What number appears most often?

Older children can add the four numbers together to get a total, and then divide the total by four to determine an average of the 4 drops. Using a calculator, children can multiply this average by 16 (the number of square boxes) to get the approximate number of stars on the sheet. Help children understand that by segmenting a larger quantity in this way they can estimate large quantities of items. Encourage them to use their frame to explore other estimates with this technique, such as the number of flecks in a floor tile, or letters on an 8- by 8-inch square of newspaper.

Across the Curriculum

🌀 **CONSTELLATION CUPS** Children can make constellation cups using paper cups and black construction paper. First, copy the constellation disk patterns to the right. Let each child choose a pattern. Have them glue their pattern to the bottom of a cup. Then, demonstrate using a sharp pencil point to make a hole through each dot in the pattern. To view their constellations, dim the lights and have children take turns pointing their cups toward a wall and shining a flashlight through the open end.

🌀 **CONSTELLATION STORIES** Share pictures and stories of the constellations. (*Glow-in-the-Dark Constellations: A Field Guide for Young Stargazers* by C.E. Thompson Putnam, 1989 is a good resource.) Then let children invent their own constellations. Give each child a sheet of dark blue construction paper and 10 star stickers. Tell children to drop the stars randomly on the paper and then stick them down them where they fall. Ask children to look at the arrangement of stars, turning the page if necessary, until they see an arrangement that could be made into the shape of an object, animal, or character. Invite them to name their "constellations" and to make up stories about them.

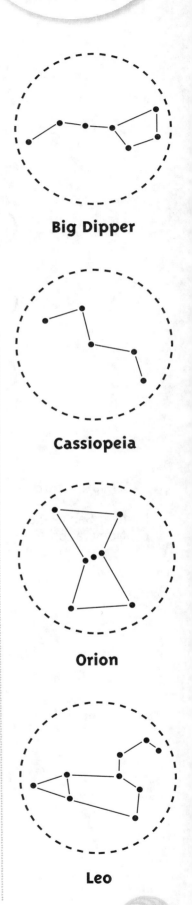

Big Dipper

Cassiopeia

Orion

Leo

Ten Black Dots

BY DONALD CREWS • *Greenwillow, 1968*

INTRODUCING THE BOOK

Through simple, colorful illustrations and rhyming verse, Donald Crews' counting book playfully portrays common objects whose parts can be seen as various numbers of black dots. For example, Crews illustrates the face of a snowman with three black dots. Read the book aloud and show children the illustrations. Discuss how the dots are used on each page. Then, ask children to name other objects that might include the given number of dots.

NCTM Standard

Number Sense and Numeration

Dotty Pictures

Materials (for each child)

- 11 pieces of 8 1/2- by 11-inch white construction paper
- 2 brass fasteners
- a plastic sandwich bag containing 55 1/2-inch colored dots or commercial stick-on dots
- glue
- crayons or markers

1 Invite children to create their own number book, similar to Crews' *Ten Black Dots*. Distribute bags of dots, glue, crayons or markers, and paper and tell children to use from one to ten dots to create their own pictures. (Older children can use greater numbers of dots, such as 20 or 50, to create pictures.) Children can label each illustrated page by writing the numeral and a sentence that includes the corresponding number word for the number of dots on the page. For example, *Four black dots can make the eyes on two cats.*

2 When children have completed their illustrations, ask them to put the pages in order from one to ten. With the last sheet of paper they can create a cover for their book, giving it a title related to their illustrations. Provide paper fasteners and help children fasten the pages into a book.

3 Invite children to share their books with classmates and their families before adding them to the class library or math center.

ACTIVITY 2 Solving Dot Equations

NCTM Standard

Concepts of Whole Number Operations

Materials

- number book pages showing from one to ten dots (from Activity 1)
- magnets or Funtak
- chalk

1 Create a simple addition problem by posting on the chalkboard two dot pictures displaying a certain number of dots on each. State a word problem and ask one child to count the dots, write a simple corresponding addition number sentence, and solve the equation. Ask another class member to check the work and then to choose two new pages to represent another addition equation.

2 Depending on the abilities of your children, you might extend the activity to incorporate a lesson on number families, inequalities, or subtraction. Children can also use three or four picture pages to create and solve equations with more than two addends.

Across the Curriculum

- **CONNECT THE DOTS** You or the children in your class can create connect-the-dot pictures by placing a piece of tracing paper over a simple picture and drawing dots with corresponding numbers in a logical sequential order. Individual connect-the-dot pictures can be duplicated and distributed to the entire class, or pictures can be laminated and placed in the math learning center, along with an erasable marker.

- **MORE COUNTING BOOKS** Provide additional examples of counting books. Invite children to read them and note the various themes used by different authors. Encourage children to make and solve equations with numbers from the books, including books with numbers in the hundreds or thousands.

"Band-Aids"

FROM *WHERE THE SIDEWALK ENDS*
BY SHEL SILVERSTEIN

Harper & Row, 1974

INTRODUCING THE POEM

Children and adults alike respond with delight to Shel Silverstein's humorous poetry. "Band-Aids" is a poem about a little boy who puts a great number of these adhesive bandages all over his body. But the end of the poem reveals that the boy has no cuts or sores! Read the poem one or more times just so children can listen for fun. Then ask children to listen and use tally marks to count the total number of Band-Aids the boy places on his body.

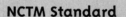

NCTM Standard

Number Sense and Numeration

ACTIVITY Bountiful Band-Aids

Materials (for each child)

- How Many Band-Aids? activity page 14
- scissors
- glue or paste
- crayons
- pencil and paper

1 Distribute a copy of the activity page to each child. Have children cut out the body and paste front to back to make a two-sided figure. Then explain that you will read the poem again; as you read, children should draw a mark to represent the correct number of Band-Aids on each of the parts of the body that are mentioned. Pause after reading each part so that children will have time to mark the reproducible with the correct number of "Band-Aids." Read the poem again when children have completed their work to help them check the number of Band-Aids they have drawn.

2 Ask children to count all of the Band-Aids and determine the total. Challenge them to figure out how many Band-Aids there would be if they added the "box full of thirty-five more."

3 Have children work in pairs to create a variety of story problems related to the Band-Aids. You may want to model a few problems first: for example, "Find the difference between the total number of Band-Aids on the feet and the total on the head." Have pairs solve their own problems. Finally, have each pair of children share their problems with the class.

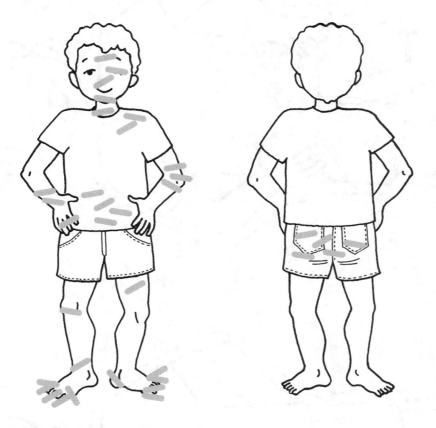

Across the Curriculum

🌀 THE BEST BANDAGES Use different brands of actual adhesive bandages and have children do some testing to see which is the strongest, which the best holding, which the best holding when wet, and so on. First have them determine what characteristic they are going to test and how they might test it, and then perform their experiments. Be sure to have them record and report on their findings.

🌀 DESIGNING BANDAGES Many adhesive bandages are colorful and decorative. Invite children to use markers or crayons to design their own bandage print or pattern that they would like to wear.

How Many Band-Aids?

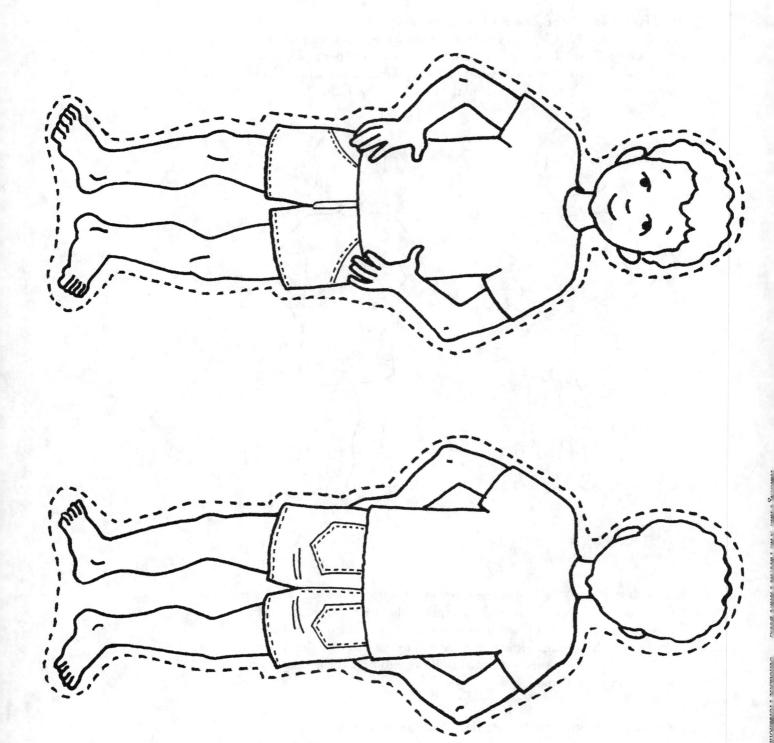

The King's Commissioners

By Aileen Friedman • *Scholastic, 1994*

INTRODUCING THE BOOK

This is the story of a king who decides he needs to count all of his commissioners to determine exactly how many he has. He receives help from his Royal Advisors, and an explanation of the Advisors' counting methods from his daughter, the princess—who comes up with a counting method of her own. As you read the story, ask children to identify the math problem and how each commissioner solved it.

ACTIVITY 1 Counting the Commissioners

NCTM Standards

Number Sense
and Numeration

Concepts of Whole
Number Operations

Materials (for each child pair)

- dried beans, pennies, or other counters
- paper and pencil

1 Ask the class to identify the many ways to count the King's Commissioners that are presented in the book. Encourage children to comment on the various counting methods used to get to 47. Discuss whether or not the ways presented made it easier or harder to find the total number of commissioners. As you reread the story, have children act out the counting methods.

2 In the story, the commissioners were counted by 2s, 5s, and 10s, with the remainder added each time. Divide the class so that each child has a partner, and give each pair 47 pieces of a selected manipulative. Have children find ways to count the manipulatives other than the ways presented in the book. Have pairs determine counting methods and then diagram each of their own methods on a piece of paper by using tally marks and circling them. For example, another way to count might be to arrange the counters in groups of 7 in order to count by 7s to 42, and then add the remaining 5.

3 When different ways have been found, have each pair of children share their findings with the class. You might record children's findings on the chalkboard and have them look for patterns.

Count By	Groups	Left Over
3	15	2
4	11	3
7	6	5

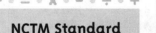

NCTM Standard

Number Sense and
Numeration

ACTIVITY 2 Multiplying With Manipulatives

Materials

☙ dried beans, pennies, or other counters

☙ paper and pencil

1 Children who are ready for beginning multiplication can use manipulatives to assist with this activity. Have children select 12 of the same manipulative. Instruct them to arrange the 12 items into rows, so that they can be counted in different ways. For instance, some children may arrange 6 rows with 2 items in each. Use this example to demonstrate how to count the number of rows and then the number of items in each row. Children will arrive at the total of 12 by counting by 6s. You can then introduce the equation, 6 x 2 = 12.

2 Have children continue to make new arrangements of the 12 items in rows. Each time, you can discuss the total in terms of sets (6 "sets" of 2, 3 "sets" of 4, and so on) or in terms of multiplication equations (6 x 2 = 12; 3 x 4 = 12; and so on). Encourage children to describe their arrangements in their own words to help with understanding.

Across the Curriculum

☙ **A SMART COMMISSIONER** Have children think of a problem they would like to have solved. Then, invite them to write a story about the problem and the commissioner who would solve the problem.

☙ **COUNTING COLLECTIBLES** Invite children to bring in collections of a variety of objects, such as shells, rocks, buttons, and so on. Have children work in small groups to determine ways to count their items.

Math Curse

BY JON SCIESZKA AND LANE SMITH • *Viking, 1995*

INTRODUCING THE BOOK

This book provides a humorous look at the uses of mathematics in everyday life: from telling time to sharing birthday cupcakes to changing money. Ask children what they think the following means: "You can think of almost everything as a math problem." Encourage them to give examples of things from the classroom setting that could be thought of in terms of a math problem. Then read *Math Curse* and have children see if any of their ideas are mentioned in the book.

ACTIVITY 1 — Math Is All Around!

NCTM Standard

Number Sense and Numeration

Materials (for each group)

- a section of a local newspaper
- a large sheet of posterboard
- scissors
- glue or paste
- markers

1 Have children brainstorm a list of the uses of math in their everyday lives. Write the list on the chalkboard and then ask children to categorize the uses under math topics. For example:

Time: Cooking, getting up, catching the school bus, going to gym class
Measurement: Weighing something, finding the length of a bookshelf
Money: Counting allowance, buying groceries, buying school lunch

2 Divide the class into groups of three or four children. Give each group a section of a recent newspaper and ask the group to examine it for uses of math. Have children cut out the examples and paste them onto posterboard in the general categories previously discussed. When posters are complete, each group can share their findings with the class. Display the posters on a "Math Is All Around!" bulletin board.

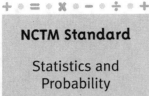

NCTM Standard

Statistics and
Probability

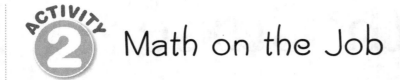

Math on the Job

ACTIVITY 2

Materials

paper and pencils

1 To increase children's awareness of the uses of mathematics in the everyday world, have each child interview an adult to find out how that person uses math in his or her occupation. Students might also bring to class math realia from each person who was interviewed. For example, a child who interviews someone who works as a homemaker might bring in a recipe or a grocery store receipt as a math artifact. A child who interviews a bus driver might bring in a copy of a route schedule.

2 Encourage children to share their findings and realia with the class, and then, as children report their findings, you might summarize the information in a table or chart and create a "Math in the Workplace" bulletin board.

Across the Curriculum

GROCERY STORY MATH Children can create word problems for their classmates based on clippings from the newspaper or from grocery store advertisements. They can cut and paste the necessary portion of the newspaper or flier onto a 5- by 8-inch index card, and then write their word problem below it. Correct answers can be written on the reverse side of the card. If you wish, you can laminate children's cards and place them in a math learning center.

SCIENCE, ANYONE? *Math Curse* ends with the statement, "You know, you can think of almost everything as a science experiment …" Explore with children sources of easy-to-do science experiments. (*A Year of Hands-on Science* and *Windowsill Science Centers*, both by Lynne Kepler [Scholastic Professional Books] are good choices.) Divide the class into small groups, and discuss with each group a simple experiment that can be easily conducted for the class. You might schedule one group per day to conduct their experiment at the beginning of science class. Or children could plan a Science Fair and invite their families to attend.

The Crayon Counting Book

BY PAM MUÑOZ RYAN AND JERRY PALLOTTA

Charlesbridge, 1996

INTRODUCING THE BOOK

In this book the authors playfully count sets of crayons by 2s, first with even and then odd numbers. The authors have also embedded in the text many words that mean two of something. Read the book aloud. During a second reading, ask children to listen for and identify those words related to two, such as *pair*, *twosome*, *couple*, *twins*, and *binary*.

ACTIVITY

Crayon Count-up!

NCTM Standards

Number Sense and Numeration

Patterns and Relationships

Materials (for the class)

✺ 210 crayons (two boxes of 96 plus 18 loose crayons) or use counters

1 Review odd and even numbers with the class. A simple way for children to tell if a number is odd or even is to put a group of crayons on a table and pair them up. If it is an even number, there will be no crayons left over. If a crayon remains, it is an odd number.

2 Walk around the room and hand out crayons. Give the first child one crayon; the second, two crayons; the third, three crayons; and so on, until you reach 20. Then tell children to line up their crayons in pairs to determine whether they have an odd or an even number.

	Odd		Even

3 ✏️✏️
   ✏️✏️

2 ✏️
   ✏️

5 ✏️✏️✏️
   ✏️✏️

4 ✏️✏️
   ✏️✏️

7 ✏️✏️✏️✏️
   ✏️✏️✏️

6 ✏️✏️✏️
   ✏️✏️✏️

3 Make a two-column chart on the chalkboard. Label one column "odd" and the other "even." Invite children, one by one, to come up to the board, choose the correct column, draw a picture of how they arranged their crayons, and write the numeral showing how many crayons they have. (Start with the child who has one crayon and go in ascending order.)

4 Ask children to examine the chart and note patterns. For example, the numbers 2, 4, 6, 8, and 0 are repeated in sequence in the even numbers; the digits 1, 3, 5, 7, and 9 are repeated in the odd numbers. Even numbers are those you say when counting by 2, and so on. Encourage children to try adding and subtracting pairs of numbers from the set of even numbers or the set of odd numbers. Ask them to make some rules about what happens when you add and subtract odd and even numbers.

Across the Curriculum

🌀 **A NUMBER WORD COLLECTION** Explain that the letters *bi-* at the beginning of a word often signal the meaning "having to do with two." Ask small groups of children to list all the words they can think of having the prefix *bi-*, such as *bicycle*, *biceps*, and *bilingual*. (Have dictionaries on hand to help them add to their lists.) Then have the class brainstorm words related to other numbers; for example, words related to three would have the prefix *tri-* and might include *tricycle*, *trio*, *triplets*, and *triangle*. Children can create poster word banks to display in the classroom, with a poster for each number. Encourage children to add words to the posters as they find new words related to numbers in books, magazines, newspapers, or other media.

🌀 **INVENT A CRAYON COLOR** Large boxes of crayons have colors with interesting and imaginative names. Give children the opportunity to invent and name a new color. Have children first wash their hands, then mix colors by putting a dab of white icing in a small catsup cup and using drops of food coloring to color it. Coffee stirrers work well to blend the colors into the icing. Have children keep track of the number of drops of each color they use and write an equation to show how they got their new color. For example: 5 drops of red + 3 drops of yellow = warm summer sun number 8. To "clean up" after this activity, give each child a few vanilla wafers on which to spread their icing.

Imogene's Antlers

BY DAVID SMALL • *Crown, 1985*

INTRODUCING THE BOOK

This is the story of Imogene and her delightful adventures when she wakes up one morning to discover that she has grown a pair of antlers. After you read the story to the class, ask children to recall the things people in the story put on Imogene's antlers. Then encourage them to discuss what they would do with a pair of antlers like Imogene's.

ACTIVITY

Antler Addition

Materials (for each child)

- 2 pipe cleaners
- 20 pieces of O-shaped oat- or fruit-flavored cereal
- paper and pencil

1 Explain to the class that they will be using pipe cleaners to create a set of small antlers. Give each child two pipe cleaners. Show them how to them bend one pipe cleaner into a V-shape. By cutting pieces of the second pipe cleaner and twisting them onto the two arms of the V, they can create antlers, as shown below.

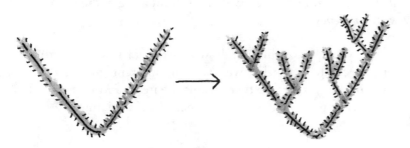

NCTM Standards

Whole Number Computation

Whole Number Operations

Number Sense and Numeration

2 Have children wash their hands. Distribute the O-shaped cereal (representing the donuts in the story) to each child. Have children work in pairs to create problems by hanging different numbers of "donuts" on each antler. They can create addition problems using the donuts on each antler as addends, and compare numbers of donuts on two antlers to create subtraction problems. If you are using colored cereal, invite children to use the colored O's in different ways. For example, children might use 2 greens and 3 greens on one side of the antlers to equal 5 oranges on the other side. Or they might designate number values to different colors: green = 1, orange = 2, and so on. Have children take turns creating antler problems for their partners to solve. Remind each pair to record all of their problems and solutions.

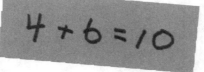

Across the Curriculum

🌀 **WHAT A CHARACTER** Share the story *The Lady With a Ship on Her Head* by Patricia Norse Lattimore (Harcourt, 1990). During a day at the beach, the main character in this story is unaware that a tiny ship has become entangled in her hair. Children will enjoy comparing and contrasting this story with *Imogene's Antlers*.

🌀 **BEYOND DONUTS** Have children draw a picture of Imogene with her antlers and decorate the antlers with an item different from any of the items mentioned in the story. Have them count the items and write an addition number sentence to show the total number of items pictured.

Domino Addition

BY LYNETTE LONG, PH.D.

Charlesbridge, 1996

▲▲▲▲▲▲▲▲▲▲▲▲▲▲▲▲▲▲▲▲▲▲▲

INTRODUCING THE BOOK

This book uses illustrations of dominoes to introduce some basic addition facts. Clear illustrations and questions (with answers provided on another page) encourage children to learn sums to 12. Readers are also encouraged to find all the dominoes that have a specific sum. Read the book and show the illustrations and discuss which facts can be represented using dominoes.

ACTIVITY 1 — Dotty Dominoes

NCTM Standards

Whole Number Operations

Whole Number Computation

Number Sense and Numeration

Materials (for each group)

- Dotty Dominoes activity page 25
- small dried beans or other counters

1 Divide the class into small groups. Give each group a Dotty Dominoes activity page and a handful of dried beans or counters. Have each child in the group select a domino and, in turn, put out beans to match the number of dots on each half of the domino.

2 As a group, children should then total the beans and record the total beneath the appropriate domino. If you wish, children can write the complete addition number sentence below each domino on the activity sheet.

NCTM Standards

Whole Number
Operations

Whole Number
Computation

Domino War

Materials

sets of dominoes made from Dotty Dominoes activity page 25

Ahead of Time

To make the dominoes more durable, copy the activity page onto sturdy paper or paste to thin cardboard or old file folders before cutting them out.

1 Divide the class into pairs. Give each pair a set of dominoes. Explain to the pairs that they will play a math game called Domino War. To play the game, children should first divide the set of dominoes into two equal sets and place both sets facedown. Each child in the pair will simultaneously turn over a domino from his or her own set. The child with the higher sum of domino dots wins both dominoes in that round. The winner of the game is the first one to collect all of the dominoes.

2 To practice higher sums, children can follow the procedure described above. When each child turns up a domino, both children must find the total of the dots on the two dominoes. The first child to say the correct sum gets both dominoes.

Across the Curriculum

DOMINO BUILDING BLOCKS Students naturally enjoy building with dominoes, as well as exploring the "domino effect." Provide center opportunities to allow this type of free play with real dominoes.

INVENTING DOMINO GAMES Teach the class how to play dominoes using the actual game rules. Also, encourage children to invent other games that can be played with a set or two of dominoes.

EDIBLE DOMINOES For a tasty math treat, let children come up with "Make My Domino" riddles that describe the dots on a domino. For example: "The dots on my domino add up to 8. There are two more dots on one side than on the other. Make my domino!" A classmate who can solve the riddle gets to make a domino with a graham cracker, peanut butter, and raisins to show the dot pattern. In this example, the domino would show 5 dots on one side and 3 on the other.

❄ **Safety Note**

Before doing this activity, check with parents about any possible food allergies your students might have.

Names: _____

Dotty Dominoes

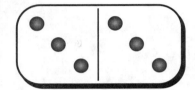

_____

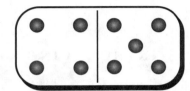

_____

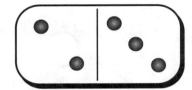

_____

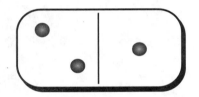

_____

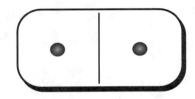

_____

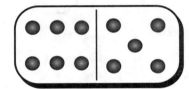

_____

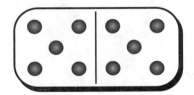

_____

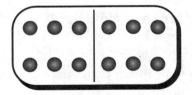

_____

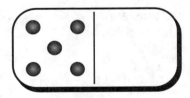

_____

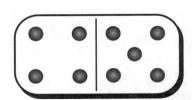

_____

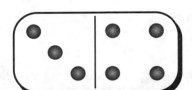

_____

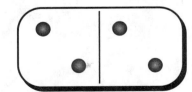

_____

Teaching Math With Favorite Picture Books   Scholastic Professional Books

The Quilt Story

BY TONY JOHNSTON AND TOMIE DEPAOLA

Putnam, 1985

INTRODUCING THE BOOK

This charming story is about a favorite quilt, beloved by a pioneer child and found many years later by one of her descendants. Read the story aloud. Then discuss how the quilt brought comfort to people and animals. Invite children to share memories of their own special quilts, blankets, or stuffed animals.

NCTM Standards

Geometry and Spatial Sense

Patterns and Relationships

 ACTIVITY

Quilt Patterns

Materials (for each child)

- 12-inch construction paper square
- 16 pieces of 3-inch construction paper squares in two contrasting colors
- scissors
- glue or paste

(for the class)

- pictures of quilts

1 Display some pictures of quilts and discuss the different kinds of quilts people make. Explain that some quilts, often called story quilts, are meant to show the progression of a story. Others show a single image. Still others show repeated patterns. Tell children they will be working in pairs to create their own pattern quilt squares with construction paper shapes.

2 Before distributing materials to children, explain that each child will make one square to contribute to a large classroom quilt. First, pairs of children should take turns making some patterns. Divide the class into pairs and distribute the materials. Tell children that they can cut some of their small squares in half along the diagonal to make triangles if they want to use shapes other than squares. One child in each pair should make a pattern by filling his or her large square with smaller squares and triangles. The other child should try to repeat that pattern. Then children exchange roles.

3 After children have made several different patterns, have them choose their favorite for their final square. They should place all the pieces, to be sure their pattern is complete, and then lift one at a time to glue or paste it down. Display the quilt squares individually or tack them together on a bulletin board to create a large classroom quilt. Ask each child to describe his or her square.

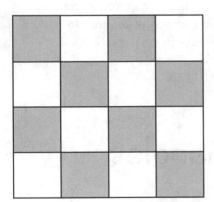
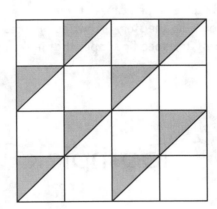
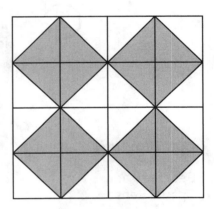

Across the Curriculum

🌀 **QUILTS IN HISTORY** Share the story *Sweet Clara and the Freedom Quilt* by Deborah Hopkinson (Knopf, 1993). Discuss how the quilt in this story was used during the time of slavery in this country to help enslaved African Americans escape to the North and find freedom.

🌀 **VISIT WITH A QUILTER** Invite a local quilt-maker to come into your classroom and show children how actual quilts are made.

🌀 **QUILTS AND MORE QUILTS!** Use the resource book *Quilting Activities Across the Curriculum* by Wendy Buchberg (Scholastic Professional Books, 1996) for more great activities related to quilts.

The Greedy Triangle

By Marilyn Burns • *Scholastic, 1994*

INTRODUCING THE BOOK

This is the story of a little triangle that has tired of its shape. The triangle visits the Shapeshifter, and becomes a four-sided figure. As the story progresses, it changes its shape several times, until it finds it was happiest being a triangle. Along the way, children are introduced to the names of polygons—from *triangle* to *dodecagon*. As you read the story, show the pictures and encourage children to identify the specific shapes that make up everyday objects.

NCTM Standard

Geometry and Spatial Sense

ACTIVITY 1 — Toothpick Triangles

Materials

- All Kinds of Triangles activity page 30
- pencils
- construction paper
- toothpicks
- glue or paste

1 Discuss the characteristics of a triangle; reinforce that a triangle is a shape with three sides and three corners, called *angles*. Distribute 10 toothpicks to each child. Invite children to make a variety of kinds of triangles, beginning with three toothpicks and then using different numbers of toothpicks to create the sides.

2 Distribute construction paper and glue and have children pick one of the triangles they've made to display. They should recreate that triangle using toothpicks and then glue it to the construction paper. Once children are finished, have them show and describe their triangles.

3 Distribute the All Kinds of Triangles activity page and encourage children to record their observations of the characteristics of the different triangles. Children can use descriptions such as: all the sides are the same size, and the corners are the same size; the bottom is bigger than the sides; one corner is bigger than the other two corners; and so on. Older children might be interested in knowing that different triangles have different names. For example, the four pictured on the activity sheet are: (1) *equilateral*, (2) *scalene*, (3) *isosceles*, and (4) *right*.

Shapes All Around

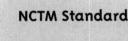

NCTM Standard

Geometry and
Spatial Sense

Materials

* drawing paper and crayons

1 Ask children to recall from the story the objects found in the everyday world and their resemblance to geometric shapes: squares, rectangles, triangles, and so on. Distribute drawing materials. Have children observe classroom objects, pick one, and then draw a geometric shape to represent it. For example, a child might pick the classroom bulletin board or door and draw a rectangular shape.

2 Once drawings are complete, invite children to play a guessing game. Let them take turns showing their shapes while the rest of the class tries to guess the actual classroom object the child has represented.

Across the Curriculum

* **SHAPE COLLAGES** Students can use magazines to find pictures of everyday objects with specific shapes. Once they have found a variety of objects, have them work together to create collages for each shape.

* **I SPY A SHAPE!** Play a game of "I Spy" to help children improve their ability to give oral descriptions using geometric shapes. Clues might look like this: "I spy something that is round. It has a glass cover. It has numbers on its face." (clock) The child who guesses correctly gives the next set of clues.

Name: _____

All Kinds of Triangles

Describe each triangle on the lines below.

1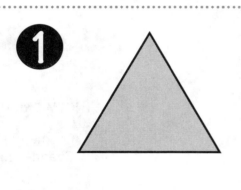

_____

_____

_____

_____

_____

2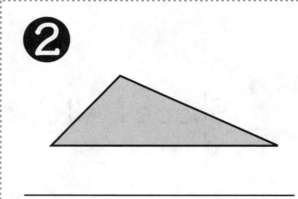

_____

_____

_____

_____

_____

3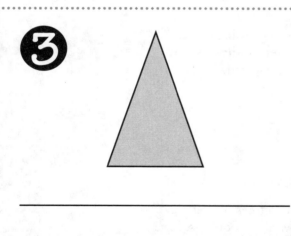

_____

_____

_____

_____

_____

4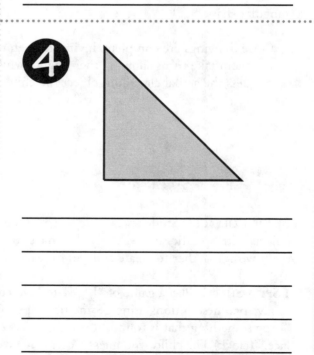

_____

_____

_____

_____

_____

Teaching Math With Favorite Picture Books   Scholastic Professional Books

Look at Annette

BY MARION WALTER

M. Evans and Company, 1971

INTRODUCING THE BOOK

This interactive book encourages children to explore symmetry. It contains a mirror that is used to alter the pictures on each two-page spread. Questions on each page help children use specific mathematical terms to move the mirror and answer questions about Annette and the things she likes. As you read the book, gather children around you so that they can take turns placing the mirror on each page.

ACTIVITY

Shape Symmetry

NCTM Standards

Geometry and
Spatial Sense

Patterns and
Relationships

Materials (for each pair)

- Symmetrical Shapes activity page 33
- plastic mirrors
- pencils

1 Demonstrate the concept of symmetry with the letters I and A on the chalkboard. Show how a line dividing each letter in half (a line of symmetry) produces two identical halves. Draw a simple house and again demonstrate symmetry by drawing a line to divide the house in half. Explain that when an object is symmetrical, a mirror can be placed on it along the line of symmetry so that the object appears whole again.

  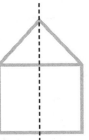

2 Divide the class into pairs and give each pair a mirror and copies of the Symmetrical Shapes activity page. Instruct children to place their mirror on each letter or picture in such a way that the entire letter can be seen when using the mirror. For example, on the letter B the mirror needs to be placed across the middle of it horizontally. Have children draw a line on each picture to show where they placed the mirror to create a complete letter or picture.

Across the Curriculum

MIRROR CODES Children will enjoy writing secret messages and using mirrors to decode them. This is done by printing backwards and then holding the paper in front of a mirror. Children will have fun experimenting to perfect the technique.

NATURE'S SYMMETRY Ask children to bring in some easily collectible objects from nature, such as leaves, flower petals, rocks, shells, and so on. By placing the edge of a pocket mirror on the center of the object or a string across the object to divide it in half, children can see whether or not the halves are exactly the same. With this information, have children classify the objects as symmetrical or not symmetrical.

Name: _____

Symmetrical Shapes

Use a mirror to find the line of symmetry for each shape. Draw the line.

W O C M

H I 8 3

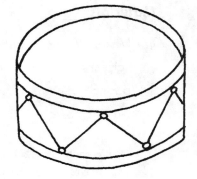

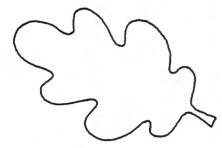

The Tangram Magician

By Lisa Campbell Ernst and Lee Ernst

Harry N. Abrams, 1990

INTRODUCING THE BOOK

In this story, the Tangram Magician changes himself into many forms. At the story's end, he encourages readers to create images of their own from the seven geometric shapes that make a tangram. After you read the story, ask children to look again at the pictures and identify some of the individual shapes that make up the forms taken by the Tangram Magician.

NCTM Standards

Geometry and Spatial Sense

Patterns and Relationships

ACTIVITY 1 — Tangram Shapes

Materials

- Make a Tangram activity page 36
- scissors
- paper
- glue or paste

1 Give each child a copy of the Make a Tangram activity page. As they cut apart the pieces, help children to identify the shapes of each of the seven pieces: two small triangles, two large triangles, one medium-sized triangle, one parallelogram, and one square.

2 Ask children to put some of the pieces into sets and to make a rule for what goes in each set. For example, children might make a set consisting of all the triangles, a set of small triangles, a set of four-sided figures, and so on.

3 Invite children to create some of the tangram figures that are illustrated in *The Tangram Magician*. Then suggest that children create some figures of their own. They might choose a favorite, paste it to another piece of paper, and label the figure.

All About Shapes

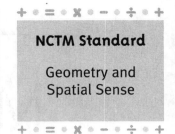

NCTM Standard

Geometry and Spatial Sense

Materials

☙ Make a Tangram and Tangram Shapes Chart activity pages 36 and 37

☙ scissors ☙ pencils

1 Distribute copies of the Make a Tangram activity page and have children cut out the seven pieces. Challenge children to reassemble their seven pieces to form the original large square.

2 Give each child a copy of the Tangram Shapes Chart. Tell children that they can work with a partner or alone to complete it, as you ask some questions. Draw attention to the shapes along the left column, and the numbers along the top. Children will use their tangram shapes to explore answers to your questions.

   Begin with a triangle. Ask: Can a triangle be made with one piece? Students then fill in the chart with their response, yes or no. Ask: Can a triangle be made with two pieces? Again, let children manipulate their pieces and then record their responses. Continue in this manner for the rest of the numbers.

3 Have children work on their own in the same way to explore the numbers of pieces needed to make a square, a rectangle, a trapezoid, and a parallelogram.

Shapes		1	2	3	4	5	6	7
Triangle	△	yes	yes	no				
Square	☐	yes	yes	no	no	no	no	yes
Rectangle	▭	no						
Trapezoid	⏢	no						
Parallelogram	▱	yes						

Across the Curriculum

☙ **TANGRAM MOSAICS** Copy the Make a Tangram activity page onto sheets of colored paper and invite children to create mosaic pictures. Children might want to arrange geometric shapes to approximate something realistic, or they may prefer to make geometric designs. Ask children to show and describe their shape mosaics when they are complete.

Name: _____

Make a Tangram

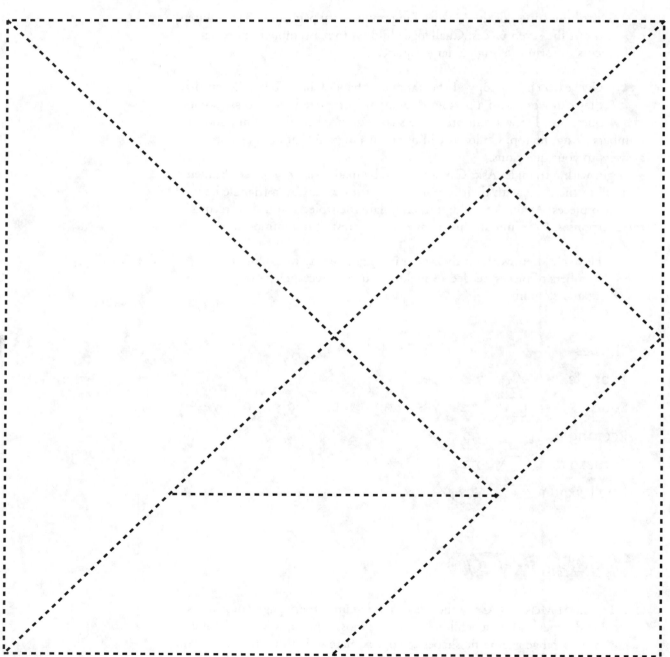

Teaching Math With Favorite Picture Books — Scholastic Professional Books

Name: _____

Tangram Shapes Chart

How many pieces can you use to make each shape? Write yes or no in each box below.

Number of Pieces

Shapes	1	2	3	4	5	6	7
triangle △							
square ▢							
rectangle ▭							
trapezoid ⏢							
parallelogram ▱							

Inch by Inch

BY LEO LIONNI

Astor-Honor Publishing, 1960

INTRODUCING THE BOOK

Students are introduced to the concept of measuring with inches through an adventuresome inchworm that measures parts of various birds. Before reading the book, ask children to show you, using their fingers, the approximate length of an inch. After reading the book, show the illustrations again and ask children to give some examples of objects that are about an inch long, such as a small paper clip.

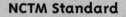

NCTM Standard

Measurement

ACTIVITY 1 — How Big Is That Animal?

Materials

* 12 one-inch pieces of green pipe cleaner
* ruler

1 Review the concepts of height, length, and width, as well as measuring to the nearest inch. Show children the pipe-cleaner pieces. Tell them that these are "inchworms." Each piece is exactly one inch long. Invite volunteers to place the inchworms end to end to measure parts of the animals portrayed in the book, such as the robin's tail, flamingo's neck, toucan's beak, heron's leg, pheasant's tail, and the entire hummingbird.

2 Record findings on the chalkboard and have children make comparison statements about the animals based upon the measurements.

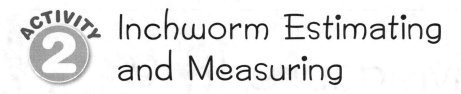

Inchworm Estimating and Measuring

NCTM Standards

Estimation

Measurement

Materials (for each child)

- Measure It! activity page 40
- 12-inch light green pipe cleaner
- 1- by 12-inch strip of green construction paper
- glue
- black marker
- pencil

1 Let children make their own Inchworm rulers. Hand out the materials listed above (except for the activity sheet) to each child. Demonstrate how to glue the pipe cleaner to the paper strip as shown. Next, show children how to use the ruler and marker to make 11 1-inch increments on the paper strip, then label the strip with the numbers 1 to 12. Remind children to line up the end of the ruler (or the first measurement mark) with the end of the paper strip.

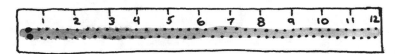

2 Then divide the class into small groups and hand out copies of the activity page. Explain that each group should work together to generate a list of classroom objects to add to the list on the chart, estimate the length, height, or circumference of each object (the Inchworm ruler will curve around round objects), and record their estimates. Then they should take turns measuring to check their estimates. Discuss strategies for rounding up or down to the nearest inch when an object falls between inch increments.

3 Once the groups are done measuring, have them compare their estimates with their results. Children can also order or graph the objects from tallest to shortest or longest to shortest using the actual measurements.

Across the Curriculum

- **COLORFUL COLLAGES** Show some illustrations from *Inch by Inch* and draw attention to Leo Lionni's use of collage, sponge paintings, and texture rubbings. Invite children to create collage paintings using manila paper, sponges, and tempera paint, simulating Leo Lionni's technique. Next, ask children to draw an outline of an animal on their collage and cut it out. Then they can paste the animals onto pieces of 8 1/2- by 11-inch posterboard. Have children exchange papers and measure one another's animals. You might also have children record information for the animal they measure in a sentence frame. See the sample, right.

Inchworm met a **[name of animal]** that measured about **[number of inches]** long and **[number of inches]** wide.

Names: _____

 # Measure It!

Things We Measured	Estimate	Actual Measurement
1 Chalkboard		
2 Bulletin Board		
3 Desk		
4		
5		
6		
7		
8		
9		
10		

Teaching Math With Favorite Picture Books   Scholastic Professional Books

The Grouchy Ladybug

BY ERIC CARLE • *Thomas Y. Crowell, 1977*

BY ERIC CARLE • *Thomas Y. Crowell, 1977*

▲▲▲▲▲▲▲▲▲▲▲▲▲▲▲▲
INTRODUCING THE BOOK
▼▼▼▼▼▼▼▼▼▼▼▼▼▼▼▼

This is the story of a tiny but very grouchy ladybug who tries to engage other animals in a fight. From daybreak until nightfall she goes from creature to creature, until she finally meets her match. Read the story aloud, and ask children what they notice about the size of the creatures the ladybug tries to fight with. Then, as you reread the story, encourage children to identify the time on each clock shown in the book. Also draw attention to the changing position of the sun in Eric Carle's illustrations.

ACTIVITY 1

How Big Is Big?

NCTM Standards

Measurement: Size

Patterns and Relationships

Materials

- reference books that have size information on the various animals listed in the story
- rulers or yardsticks
- string or yarn
- masking tape
- markers

1 Divide the class into groups of four or five children. Explain that each group is to choose one of the animals from the story and find out its actual size. Help each group use the reference books to find the size of their creature. Then go outside on the playground or to the gym and have groups use rulers or yardsticks to lay out a piece of string or yarn the length of their animal. Use a piece of tape to designate a starting line at which each group should begin to measure, so that you will be able to compare lengths.

2 When measurements are completed, have the groups arrange the lengths of string or yarn from smallest to largest. Ask each group to label their string with the name and length of their animal. Talk with children about the relative sizes of the animals.

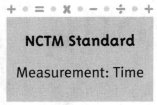

NCTM Standard

Measurement: Time

A Whale of a Time

Materials

🌀 large classroom demonstration clock

🌀 drawing paper

🌀 crayons or pastels

1 Using the pages from *The Grouchy Ladybug*, have volunteers tell the hour from each clock shown, up to the ladybug's encounter with the whale at 5 o'clock. As one child tells the time, have another child model the time on the demonstration clock. Then work in the same way with times to the half hour and to fifteen minutes. Students might also use clocks made with patterns from the Paper Plate Clock activity page 55, so that each child can model the time.

2 Distribute paper and drawing materials. Invite each child to choose a time of day, draw a clock showing that time, and then draw something the ladybug might do at that time. Their ideas may be realistic or fanciful.

Across the Curriculum

🌀 LIVELY LADYBUGS! Obtain some live ladybugs for your children to observe. They can be collected or purchased from a supplier such as Insect Lore by calling 1-800-LIVE-BUG. Make simple bug habitats by placing leaves and small rocks in a jar. Place the ladybugs in the containers, fix a piece of nylon pantyhose over the top of the jar with a rubber band, and have the class observe and record information about the bugs' behavior. Afterward, release the ladybugs outdoors.

🌀 BUGGY CRAFTS Use play clay to create ladybug jewelry or paperweights. If clay is not available, you can use this simple recipe for making your own:

2 cups all purpose flour
1 cup salt
1 cup water
1 teaspoon vegetable oil
food coloring (optional)

Mix together flour, salt, water, and oil. If the dough is too sticky, add more flour, one tablespoon at a time. If you wish, add drops of food coloring until you obtain a desired color. After the bugs dry, children can paint and decorate them with arts and crafts supplies such as sequins and wiggly eyes.

Alexander, Who Used to Be Rich Last Sunday

BY JUDITH VIORST • *Atheneum, 1978*

INTRODUCING THE BOOK

This is the humorous story of how Alexander, a little boy who just can't seem to save his money, spends the dollar his grandparents have given him. After you read the story aloud, encourage children to react to the ways Alexander spends his money. Encourage them to discuss what they would do with a dollar.

ACTIVITY 1 — One Hundred Cents

NCTM Standards

Measurement: money

Concepts of Whole Number Operations

Fractions and Decimals

Materials (for each child)

- $1.00 = 100 Cents activity page 45
- pencil or marker
- scissors
- tape

1 Distribute two copies of the activity page to each child. Begin by having children cut out and assemble the ten strips to obtain one long strip with one hundred pennies. Then review with children that one dollar is the same as 100 pennies, or 100 cents.

2 Explain that you will reread the story of Alexander. Tell children that as Alexander spends his money in the story they should count off pennies to subtract that amount of money. Help children "convert" coins such as nickels, dimes, or quarters to an equivalent number of pennies. At the conclusion of the story, they will discover that they have counted off 100 pennies, showing that Alexander has indeed spent all his money.

3 For older children, you can distribute play money and have children use pennies, nickels, dimes, and quarters to represent in different ways each amount of money Alexander spent or lost in the story. For example, Alexander spends twenty cents at a garage sale. Students could represent that amount with coins such as 2 dimes, 1 dime and 2 nickels, 1 dime and 10 pennies, 20 pennies, 3 nickels and 5 pennies, or 1 nickel and 15 pennies.

Make a Money Chart

Materials (for each child)

- $1.00 = 100 Cents activity page 45
- scissors
- tape
- glue or paste
- large piece of construction paper

1 Distribute two copies of the activity page to each child and have children cut and assemble a strip to represent 100 pennies. Then post a list of the items Alexander bought and the places he lost his money, with the amount spent or lost next to each. Have children cut strips off their long strip of 100 pennies to show the number of cents for each amount. Students can paste their strips on the piece of construction paper to make a chart showing amounts of money, from greatest to least. Then have them label each strip with what Alexander spent the money on.

2 Once the charts are completed, encourage children to use them to make true statements about the information. For example, "Alexander spent 4 cents more on gum than he spent for the candy bar;" or "Alexander spent the same amount for kicking his brother and saying bad words as he did for gum."

How did Alexander spend his dollar?

candle, teddy bear, cards 20¢
gum 15¢
lost bet with mom 15¢
snake rental 12¢
candy 11¢
fine for saying bad words 10¢
lost money 8¢
fine for kicking brother 5¢
lost money in magic trick 4¢

Alexander spent 4 cents more on gum than he spent for the candy bar.

Across the Curriculum

- **AREN'T WE SMART?** Compare the poem "Smart" by Shel Silverstein, from the book *Where the Sidewalk Ends,* to the story of Alexander. Help children create a chart to compare ways the main character of the story and that of the poem are alike and ways they are different.

NCTM Standards

Measurement: Money

Statistics and Probability

Fractions and Decimals

$1.00 = 100 cents

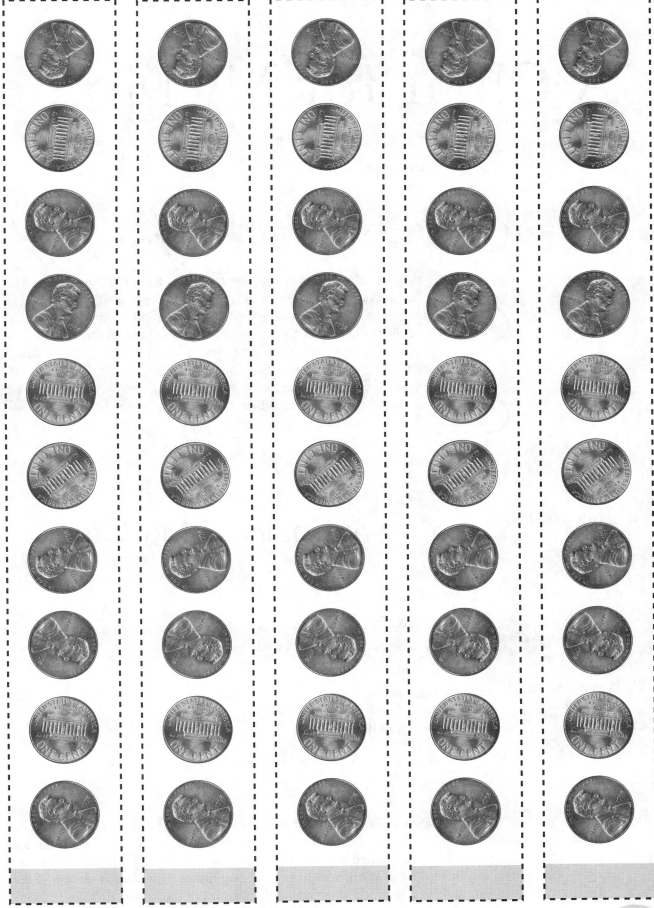

A Chair for My Mother

BY VERA B. WILLIAMS

Greenwillow, 1982

INTRODUCING THE BOOK

This Caldecott Honor Book presents the story of a family that saves coins in a jar to buy a new chair after losing all of their possessions in a fire. Before you read the story, ask children to describe the kind of chair they would dream of having, for themselves or for someone in their family. After reading the story, ask children if they have ever saved their money for a long time to buy something special, as the family in the story did. Invite children to discuss the things they saved for and how long it took to have the right amount of money to buy the item.

NCTM Standards

Measurement: Money

Fractions and Decimals

Whole Number Computation

Number Sense and Numeration

ACTIVITY · A Chair of My Own

Materials (for each pair)

- furniture catalogs, mail order catalogs, or advertising circulars showing different kinds of chairs and their prices
- 2 number cubes
- play money

(for each child)

- A Chair of My Own activity page 48
- paper and pencil

1 Divide the class so that each child works with a partner. Distribute the catalogs and circulars and a copy of the activity page to each child. First have children look through the catalogs to find a chair that they would like to "buy." Instruct them to note the price of their chair at the top of the activity page. Help them round the amount to the nearest dollar.

2 Explain that children will play a game with their partner to "earn" money to "purchase" their chair. Each pair gets two number cubes and a supply of play money. The first player rolls one number cube and then the other; the amount is read in the order of the roll. For example, if the player rolls 3 and then 6, he or she has earned $36.00. The player records that amount under Week 1. As players take turns rolling the number cubes, whatever number they roll is the number of dollars they can collect. Children continue rolling the number cubes, recording their "weekly pay," and totaling the money they have earned until they reach enough to buy their chair. The first player to reach the necessary amount wins.

3 After the game is finished, ask children to discuss how long it took before they had enough money for their chairs. Compare this to how long it might actually take to earn enough for the chair.

Across the Curriculum

* **MY DREAM CHAIR** Provide a variety of arts and crafts materials (craft sticks, boxes, yarn, fabric scraps, and so on) for children to create a small-scale model of their "dream chair." Ask children to write a description of their special chair on a large index card that will be placed next to their chair model. Display the finished chairs on a table with a sign, "Best Seats in the House."

* **EARN AND LEARN** Give the class an opportunity to brainstorm something they might enjoy earning and saving money to get or to give. Then, make a list of ways to earn the money. If possible, have children put their ideas to work to actually purchase the item or make a contribution to a local group or cause.

Name: _____

A Chair of My Own

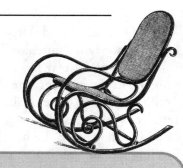

Cost of My Chair $ _____

Number	Cube Roll	Money "Earned"
Week 1		
Week 2		
Week 3		
Week 4		
Week 5		
Week 6		
Week 7		
Week 8		
Week 9		
Week 10		
Week 11		
Week 12		
Week 13		
Week 14		
Week 15		
Week 16		
Week 17		
Week 18		
Week 19		
Week 20		

Teaching Math With Favorite Picture Books   Scholastic Professional Books

Pigs Will Be Pigs

By Amy Axelrod • *Four Winds Press, 1994*

Introducing the Book

In this story, the Pig family members are hungry—but there is nothing good to eat at home. They realize that they need money to buy food, so they make a housewide search. Eventually the Pig family finds enough money to go out to their favorite restaurant.

After the first reading, you might discuss times that children and their families have conducted a similar search and compare some likely locations where money could be found. As you share the story during a second reading, have children guess how much money the pigs found and then keep a running total to find the actual amount.

ACTIVITY 1

Restaurant Orders

NCTM Standards

Measurement: Money

Whole Number Computation

Fractions and Decimals

Materials

- Guest Check and Menu activity pages 51–52
- pencils
- play money (optional)

1 Divide the class into pairs and give each child a copy of a Guest Check and Menu activity page. Explain to children that with their partner they will take turns pretending they are servers and customers. The customers should use the menu to select items they would like to order. The servers will write up the selections on the order form, add the amount owed, and the customer will check the server's total. Children might also use play money to act out paying and receiving change.

2 Invite children to role-play a restaurant again, but this time specify conditions for the menu order. For example, they might have only $17.34 (one half of the amount of money the pigs found) or $8.67 (one quarter of the amount of money the pigs found) to spend. Afterward, have partners share with the class the different kinds of food they ordered given the amount available.

NCTM Standards

Measurement:
Money

Whole Number
Computation

Fractions and
Decimals

Shopping Problems!

Materials

🍥 paper and pencils

🍥 grocery store ads

1 Begin this activity with the whole class by modeling a sample word problem. For example, you might tell the class that Mrs. Pig has $23.00 to go grocery shopping. She goes to the store and gets milk ($1.50), bread ($1.30), two candy bars ($.50 each), and a chicken ($3.50). Write the problem conditions on the chalkboard as you tell the word problem. Then ask the class to determine how much money Mrs. Pig spent at the grocery store, and how much she had left. Discuss as a group how to solve the problem. Ask individual children to give their solutions and methods for obtaining them.

2 Explain to the class that they will be creating their own word problems based on the characters from *Pigs Will Be Pigs*. Distribute grocery store advertisements. Have each child create a word problem and solve it on a separate sheet of paper. Ask each child to exchange his or her problem with a classmate. The problem writers should compare answers with the answers of the problem solvers to see if the correct answer was found.

Across the Curriculum

🍥 MY FAVORITE MENU Have children bring in a variety of menus from local restaurants and compare the prices. Discuss the types of food on each menu and talk with children about the factors that help determine the prices, such as competition, location, type of restaurant, and so on.

Guest Check

Order	How Many?	Amount

Guest Check

Order	How Many?	Amount

Name: _____

Menu

Appetizers

Nachos with salsa	$1.50
Stuffed jalapeños	$2.00

Salads

Salad bar (with dinner)	$1.95
Salad bar only	$5.00

House Specials

Cheese enchiladas	$5.00
Beef enchiladas	$5.50
Chicken enchiladas	$5.50
Bean burritos	$4.00

Pizza

Large	$6.50
Small	$4.00

Side Dishes

Rice	$1.00
Refried beans	$2.00

Desserts

Flan	$1.95
Fried ice cream	$2.50
Fresh fruit	$2.00

Beverages

Cola	$1.00
Frozen fruitee	$2.00
Milk	$1.00
Iced tea	$1.00
Juice	$1.25

Teaching Math With Favorite Picture Books   Scholastic Professional Books

Time to...

BY BRUCE MCMILLAN • *Lothrop, Lee & Shepard, 1989*

INTRODUCING THE BOOK

This is a photo essay of a typical day in a child's life, from rising to bedtime. As you read the story, show each two-page spread. Ask children to note the time shown on both the analog and the digital clock. Talk about things the child in the story does throughout the day. Then encourage children to tell what they do at those times of day.

What Time Is It?

NCTM Standards

Measurement: Time

Fractions and Decimals

Patterns and Relationships

Materials

- Paper Plate Clock activity page 55
- scissors
- 9-inch paper plates
- brass fasteners
- demonstration clocks (analog and digital)
- Digital Clock activity page 56
- thin cardboard or old file folders
- glue or paste

Ahead of Time

Poke a hole in the center of each paper plate so that children can insert a brass fastener.

1 Review telling time to the hour, half hour, and quarter hour. Relate different ways to say the same time, emphasizing words related to fractions. For example, 3:15 is the same as "quarter after three." 9:30 is the same as "half past nine." By showing these times on the demonstration clock as you say them, you can provide a very visual way for children to relate quarter hours and half hours to the fractional parts 1/2 and 1/4.

2 Give each child a paper plate, a copy of the Paper Plate Clock activity page, scissors, and a brass fastener. Have children cut out the clock and the minute and hour hands, and then assemble the clock as shown on the next page.

- Put the clock face, then the minute hand, and then the hour hand on top of the paper plate.
- Align the dot at the center of the clock pattern over the hole in the plate.
- Poke the brass fastener through the dot at the center of the clock face and through the dot on each of the hands to attach them.

3 Have children work in pairs or small groups, taking turns calling a time and showing the given time on their paper plate clocks. Older children can work to smaller time intervals, such as 4:10 or 1:25 or 7:57.

4 Then, help children compare reading an analog clock with reading a digital clock by letting each child make a model of a digital clock. Give each child a copy of the Digital Clock activity page, scissors, thin cardboard, and glue or paste. Show them how to assemble the clock as follows:

- Glue the activity page to thin cardboard. Then cut out the clock pattern, the number strips, and the a.m./p.m. strip.
- Paste together the pieces of the 1 to 12 number strip and the 00 to 59 number strip. Each should form one long strip.
- Cut slits as shown in the clock pattern. Slide the number strips through the slits in the clock. Do the same thing with the a.m./p.m. strip. Glue together the ends of each strip to make a loop as shown.
- To change the time, gently pull on each loop until the desired number appears.

5 Repeat step 3 above and have children show the time using both clocks.

Across the Curriculum

🌀 MARCHING IN TIME Obtain a tape of a song with a clock or time theme, such as "Rock Around the Clock" and a portable cassette player. On 12 sheets of paper, write the numerals 1 to 12. Go outside and set the numerals on the ground in a large circle, so that they look like a clock. Have children stand around the outside of the circle. Tell them that when the music starts they should walk slowly in a clockwise direction around the circle. Start and stop the music periodically. When the music stops, call a time, such as 4 o'clock. The children standing at "12" and "4" raise their hands. Continue to play in this manner, starting and stopping the music and calling a time. Then change to half-hour intervals, fifteen-minute intervals, and so on.

Name: _____

Paper Plate Clock

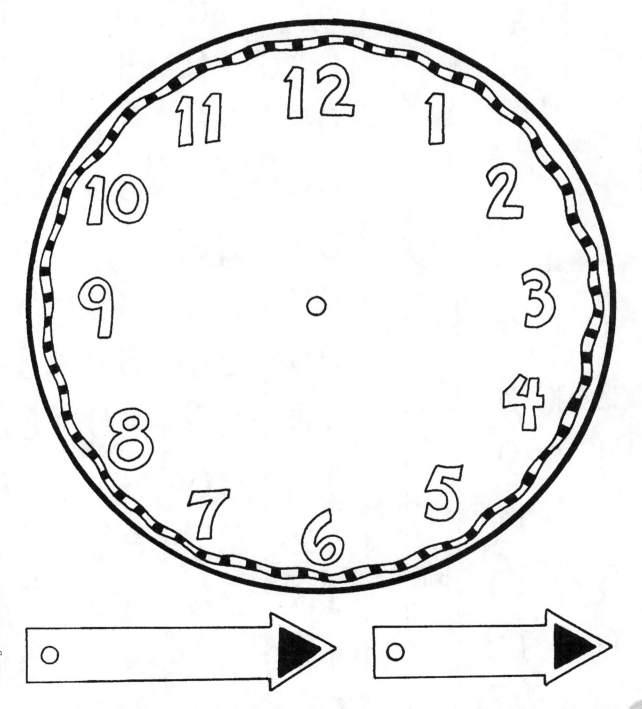

Digital Clock

1	7	
2	8	a.m.
3	9	
4	10	
5	11	p.m.
6	12	

00	15	30	45
01	16	31	46
02	17	32	47
03	18	33	48
04	19	34	49
05	20	35	50
06	21	36	51
07	22	37	52
08	23	38	53
09	24	39	54
10	25	40	55
11	26	41	56
12	27	42	57
13	28	43	58
14	29	44	59

Teaching Math With Favorite Picture Books Scholastic Professional Books

The M&M's® Brand Chocolate Candies Counting Book

BY BARBARA BARBIERI MCGRATH • *Charlesbridge Publishers, 1994*

INTRODUCING THE BOOK

*T*he M&M's® *Brand Chocolate Candies Counting Book* takes children beyond counting into simple addition and subtraction, forming sets, and shape recognition. McGrath's colorful illustrations and use of rhyming text add to the overall appeal of the book. With a small bag of M&M's at hand, read the book aloud. Have volunteers demonstrate the activities described in the book.

ACTIVITY 1  Candy Sort

NCTM Standards

Statistics and Probability

Estimation

Number Sense and Numeration

Concepts of Whole Number Operations

Materials (for each pair)

🌀 Inside a Bag of M&M's activity page 59

🌀 one small bag of M&M candies

1 Have children work in pairs. Begin by giving each pair a copy of the activity page and a small bag of M&M candies. Ask them to estimate the total number of candies in the bag. Have children record their estimates on the activity sheet. Keeping that total in mind, ask them to guess how many candies of each color are in the bag. Have children record their guesses as well.

2 Have children wash their hands. Then they can open the bags of candy and count the total number of pieces contained in the bag. Children record that number and compare the actual count to estimates they made earlier.

3 Tell children to sort the candy by color and count the number of each. Students then record and compare these counts to their estimates. Discuss children's findings. For example: Did all of the bags contain the same number of candies? Did all the bags contain the same number of each color? Which color appeared most often? Which color appeared least often?

ACTIVITY 2 Candy Number Sentences

Materials (or each group)

☙ plastic sandwich bag

☙ M&M candies

☙ paper and pencils

Ahead of Time

❋ **Safety Note**

Before doing this activity, check with parents about any possible food allergies your students might have.

Prepare for each group of children a plastic sandwich bag of M&M's containing some of each color.

1 Have children wash their hands. Divide the class into small groups and give each group a bag of M&M's. Have them empty the M&M's onto a clean piece of paper on a table or desk and then sort the candies and record the number of each color.

2 Explain that children will be solving math problems using the numbers they have recorded for their candy colors. Choose a group to tell you the number of red and the number of brown M&M's they found in their bag. On the chalkboard, write a number sentence that corresponds to their numbers, such as 3 [red] + 7 [brown] = _____ and ask children to complete the sentence. After doing several more examples, have children create and solve their own addition and subtraction problems using their numbers from the M&M's sorting. In turn, each child in the group can say a number sentence and the others in the group can check to see if it is correct.

Across the Curriculum

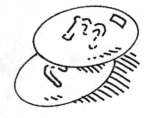

☙ MAKE MINE MAUVE Have children write persuasive letters to the M&M's candy company, in which they argue to replace their least favorite color of candy with another color of their choice. An alternative to writing individual letters would be to have children, as a class, vote on the color to be replaced and the color to be added. Students can dictate their arguments and a class letter could be composed and sent to the company.

Name: _____

Inside a Bag of M&M's

Estimates	Actual Numbers and Colors
_____ Total Number	_____ Total Number
_____ Blue	_____ Blue
_____ Yellow	_____ Yellow
_____ Orange	_____ Orange
_____ Brown	_____ Brown
_____ Green	_____ Green
_____ Red	_____ Red

A Three Hat Day

BY LAURA GERINGER • *HarperCollins, 1985*

▲▲▲▲▲▲▲▲▲▲▲▲▲
INTRODUCING THE BOOK

R.R. Pottle the Third comes from a family of collectors. He loves hats and owns a sizable collection of them. One day when he is sad, R.R. Pottle puts on three hats at once. He sets out for a walk and finds the perfect woman to be his wife—a woman who also loves hats! After you read the story aloud, invite children to talk about types of collections they or members of their families have. Discuss ways to count and organize collections.

+ = • ✕ • – • ÷ + +

NCTM Standards

Statistics and Probability

Patterns and Relationships

+ = • ✕ • – • ÷ + +

A Hat Sort

Materials:

🌀 Hats Off! activity page 62

🌀 crayons or markers

🌀 scissors

🌀 yarn or string

1 Give each child a copy of the Hats Off! activity page. Have them color and cut out the hats. Ask several children to show one of their hats and describe its characteristics.

2 Gather children in a circle and place two overlapping yarn or string circles on the floor to create a large Venn diagram. Ask a volunteer to give you a hat. Place it in one of the circles and ask other children to describe it. From another child take a hat that has a different characteristic and place it in the other circle. Explain that the circles are for sets of (for example) red hats and hats with buckles. Invite children in turn to select one of their hats and place it where it belongs in the Venn diagram. As hats that are red and have a buckle are offered, help children see that they belong in the overlapping part of the circles, because they have characteristics of both sets.

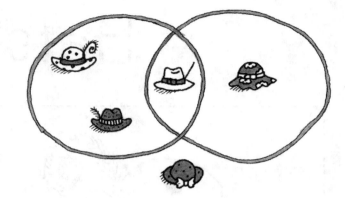

3 Talk with children about what to do with hats that have neither of the characteristics: for example, a green hat or a hat with a feather. (These should be placed outside of the yarn circles.)

Hats Off!

Materials (for each pair)

- Hats Off! activity page 62
- crayons
- scissors
- small paper bag
- paper and pencils

1 Divide the class into pairs. Give each pair of children a copy of the activity page, crayons, a bag, scissors, and paper and pencils. Ask children to color the hats as they choose, and then to cut out the hats and put two in the paper bag—one hat with a feather and one without. Ask what could happen when one hat is picked from the bag. Help children to recognize that either a hat with a feather or a hat without a feather could be picked.

2 Have pairs work together to play a prediction game. One child adds one more hat to the bag without letting his or her partner see it. The partner predicts what could happen when a hat is picked. Then the partner picks a hat and uses a tally mark to record whether it is a hat with or without a feather. The hat is placed back in the bag, and the partner makes another pick. After ten picks and tallies, the partner predicts what the combination of hats is in the bag: 2 hats with feathers and 1 without, or 1 with feathers and 2 without. The first child reveals the hats. Then children reverse roles.

3 After several rounds, talk with children about how they made their predictions. After ten picks, were they always right about the combination in the bag? Did they get better at making predictions that turned out to be correct?

+ • = • ✗ • − • ÷ • +

NCTM Standards

Statistics and Probability

Patterns and Relationships

+ • = • ✗ • − • ÷ • +

Hats With Feathers	Hats Without Feathers
III	HHT II

Across the Curriculum

- HATS IN THE NEWS! Use newspaper and masking tape to create paper hats. Place two sheets of newspaper over a child's head and create a band around the crown with masking tape. Then start from the edge of the paper and roll it toward the masking tape band to create a brim. Children can paint or decorate their hats with a variety of arts-and-crafts materials such as sequins, feathers, and ribbon.

Hats Off!

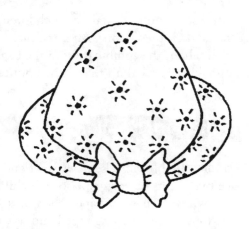

Teaching Math With Favorite Picture Books   Scholastic Professional Books

Hanukkah!

BY RONI SCHOTTER • *Little, Brown, 1990*

▲▲▲ INTRODUCING THE BOOK ▲▲▲

This charming Hanukkah story introduces children to traditions of the holiday, including favorite foods and the dreidel game. As you read, encourage children who celebrate Hanukkah to compare their celebration with that of the family in the story.

ACTIVITY

The Dreidel Game

NCTM Standard

Statistics and Probability

Materials (for each child)

- Make a Dreidel! activity page 65
- tagboard
- scissors
- glue or tape
- sharpened pencil
- unsharpened pencil with eraser
- small dried beans or counters

1 Invite children to play the traditional dreidel game. To make a dreidel, distribute a copy of the Make a Dreidel! activity page to each child. Have children follow the directions on the activity page, along with you, to assemble their dreidels. (Let each child make a dreidel to take home although only one will be needed for each group to play.)

2 Divide the class into groups of three or four. Each group needs one dreidel. Each player gets 20 counters.

Nun means "take none." The player does nothing and the next player takes a turn.

Gimel means "take all." Any time a player spins *Gimel*, the player takes all of the counters and then all players must put one into the pot before the game can continue.

Heh (hay) means "take half." If a player rolls *Heh*, the player takes half of the counters from the pot. (If there's an odd number of counters in the pot, the player takes one extra.)

Shin means "put in one." The player puts one counter into the pot.

3 Review the Hebrew letters on the dreidel (left). To begin the game, each child should put one counter into the "pot." Then one player begins by spinning the dreidel. When it stops, the player follows the direction that lands faceup. Then the next player spins and the game continues in this fashion.

4 When a player is out of counters, he or she is out of the game. The winner is the player who has won everything from the others.

Across the Curriculum

🌀 **PLAN A HANUKKAH PARTY!** Ask children to bring in, or locate in a cookbook, a recipe for *latkes* (potato pancakes) and make them with the class. Then share another delightful Hanukkah story, *Latkes and Applesauce* by Fran Manushkin (Scholastic, 1992).

🌀 **WORKING BY CANDLELIGHT**
Have children report on the lighting of Hanukkah candles. Ask them to calculate how many candles are lit during the eight nights of Hanukkah.

Make a Dreidel!

1 Cut out the pattern along the solid lines. Paste the pattern to lightweight cardboard.

2 Fold on the dotted lines, making sharp creases.

3 Use a sharp pencil point to make a hole through each ●.

4 Glue or tape together the dreidel as shown.

5 Push an unsharpened pencil through the dreidel with the eraser tip down.

6 Spin the dreidel and adjust the amount of eraser showing so that the dreidel will spin easily.

Shin

Heh

Gimel

Nun

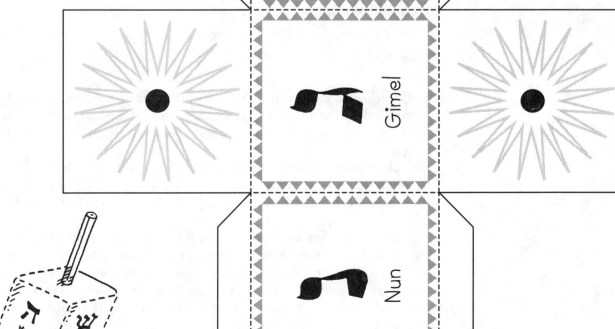

Teaching Math With Favorite Picture Books   Scholastic Professional Books

Ed Emberley's Picture Pie

A Circle Drawing Book BY ED EMBERLEY • *Little, Brown, 1984*

INTRODUCING THE BOOK

Ed Emberley's books delight children by showing art created from simple shapes. In *Picture Pie*, Emberley shows how, by dividing circles into pie-shaped segments, a variety of pictures can be created. The book also shows details for duplicating some of the *Picture Pie* illustrations. As you share the book, focus on the fractional parts of circles used to create the pictures.

NCTM Standards

Fractions and Decimals

Geometry and Spatial Sense

Fraction Pictures

Materials

- Circle Fractions activity page 67
- large sheets of construction paper
- scissors
- glue sticks or paste
- crayons or markers

1 Give children each a copy of the activity page and have them cut out the circles along the dotted lines. They should have one whole circle, and five circles divided respectively into halves, thirds, fourths, sixths, and eighths.

2 Have children use their fraction parts to explore equivalent fractions, for example, how many of each fraction make one whole, how many of each fraction make one half, how many eighths make one fourth, and so on.

3 Divide the class into small groups. The children in each group can combine their circles into a common pile. Give each group a sheet of construction paper, glue sticks or paste, and crayons or markers. Explain that each group should create a picture using the circle parts. As they are working, children may wish to consult some of Ed Emberley's shape figures, or they may want to create something entirely different. When each group finishes their picture, they should total the number of whole circles used to make it and then describe their picture to the class.

Name: _____

Circle Fractions

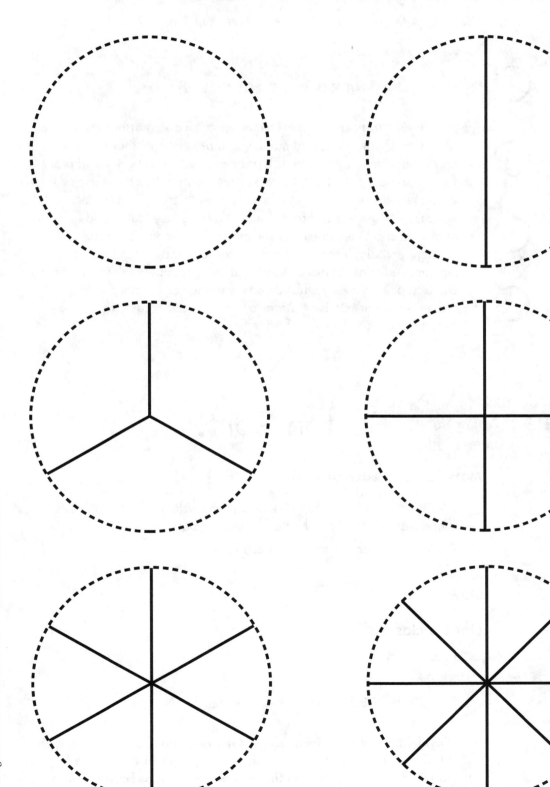

Billy's Button

BY WILLIAM ACCORSI • *Greenwillow, 1992*

INTRODUCING THE BOOK

*B*illy's Button encourages children to think about attributes such as size, shape, color, and number of buttonholes as they look at illustrations to find the buttons that belong to Billy. (Check your library for this unusual out-of-print title.) Before reading the book, have children examine their own clothing to discover whose clothing has buttons. Ask volunteers to use words that describe the size, shape, color, and number of buttonholes to tell about characteristics of their own buttons.

Then read aloud the first page of the story and ask children to summarize the attributes of Billy's button. Continue reading and have children point out Billy's button on each page of the story. During rereading, point to other buttons on each page and ask why those buttons could not be Billy's button.

NCTM Standard

Patterns and Relationships

Button Sort!

Materials (for each group)

🌀 a self-closing plastic bag filled with ten buttons of varying sizes, shapes, colors, and number of holes per button

🌀 8 1/2- by 11-inch sheet of posterboard

🌀 glue

🌀 markers

(for the class)

🌀 hole punch

🌀 3 "O" rings

🌀 2 8 1/2- by 11-inch sheets of posterboard

1 Divide the class into small groups. Give each group a plastic bag with 10 buttons of varying colors, sizes, shapes, and number of holes. Ask children to select a particular button that will be their group's button, and have the group write a set of characteristics that distinguish it from other buttons in the collection. Have children glue the assortment of buttons onto the top half of the sheet of posterboard and write the characteristics below, following the model presented in the book. See the example, right.

2 Have each group share their page with the class and read the characteristics of their group's button. The rest of the class should try to guess the button being described. Collect the pages to make a Class Button Book. Use the extra sheets of posterboard to make a front and back cover. Stack together the pages, punch holes along the left side, and assemble the book using "O" rings.

Our button is round.
Our button has no dots.
Our button is not green or purple.
Our button has 4 holes.
Our button is not all one color.
Find our button.

Group 2. Luis, Angela, Matt, Ellen

ACTIVITY 2 Guess My Button

+ • = • x • - • ÷ • +

NCTM Standard

Patterns and Relationships

+ • = • x • - • ÷ • +

Materials

 an assortment of different buttons

1 Explain to the class that they will play a "Guess My Button" game, similar to the game Twenty Questions. Invite each child to select a button from a container of buttons, without letting the other members of the class see it.

2 Choose one child to start the game. Other children will ask questions about that child's button that can be answered with a yes or no. For example, they can ask questions such as: "Is the button round?" "Is the button red?" "Does it have two holes?" A maximum of twenty questions per round can be asked about a particular button. You might appoint one child to keep a count of the number of questions asked.

3 When a child thinks he or she can accurately draw the button's shape, size, color, and number of holes, a guess is made. If the guess is incorrect, the game continues until a correct guess is made or twenty questions have been asked. If the guess is correct, that child is next to choose a button and answer questions from the class.

Across the Curriculum

 BUTTON NECKLACES Children can explore patterns by making button necklaces, bracelets, or pins that display a distinct sequence or pattern, creating such patterns as small, round, two-holed red; small, round, three-holed blue; large, rectangular, four-holed yellow; and so on. Children can show their creations to other classmates and challenge them to discover the pattern.

Caps for Sale

By Esphyr Slobodkina • *Harper & Row, 1947*

INTRODUCING THE BOOK

The old saying, "Monkey see, monkey do" is illustrated in this tale that has become a classic. A cap peddler, having a slow day, sits down under a tree to nap. While he sleeps, a pack of monkeys each takes one of his caps. But by a happy accident, he gets them all back. Read the story through once. As you reread it, encourage children to chime in on repeated sentences or the monkeys' reply of "tsz, tsz, tsz" to the frustrated peddler.

NCTM Standard

Patterns and Relationships

Stack-the-Caps Patterns

Materials (for each pair)

- Stack-the-Caps activity page 72
- gray, blue, brown, and red crayons
- paste or glue
- scissors
- construction paper

1 Divide the class into pairs. Give each pair of children an activity page, scissors, and crayons. Have children color the peddler's caps: 4 blue, 4 brown, 4 gray, and 4 red, and then cut them out along with the peddler pattern.

2 Explain that the pairs will play a pattern guessing game. To begin playing, the first child creates a pattern by stacking caps on the peddler's head. The second child observes and describes the pattern, then looks away. The partner changes something by rearranging or disrupting the pattern. Once the change is made, the observer turns back and tries to identify the change in order to recreate the original pattern. Then children change roles and repeat the activity.

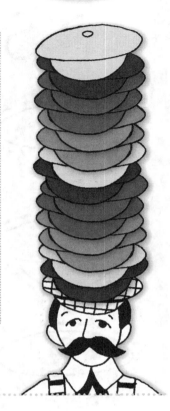

3 At the end of the game, ask each pair to choose a pattern and paste the peddler wearing his caps onto a piece of construction paper. Display the patterns and have the class identify each one.

Across the Curriculum

✿ **A MONKEY ROLE-PLAY** Copy and enlarge the pattern here and help children use it to make construction paper caps—some each of gray, blue, brown, and red, and one that is checkered. Use brass fasteners to attach a construction paper band to either side of the visor. Adjust to fit on children's heads. Reread *Caps for Sale* and have one child play the role of the peddler while the others play the monkeys. Have them use their cap visors to reenact the hat scenes.

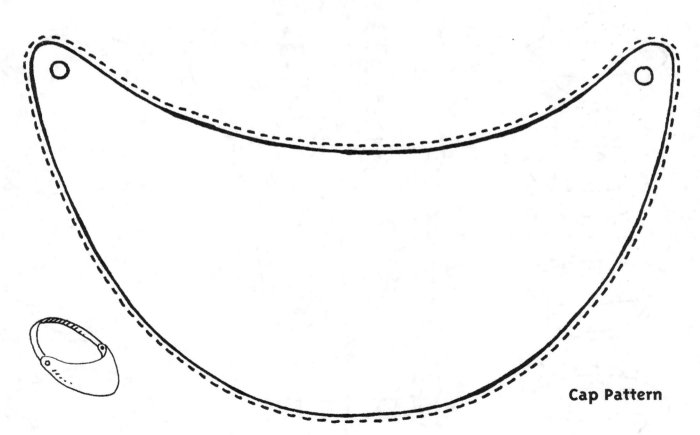

Cap Pattern

Stack-the-Caps

Jump, Frog, Jump

By Robert Kalan • *Greenwillow, 1981*

INTRODUCING THE BOOK

This is a cumulative story about a frog and a series of other animals. As you read the story, encourage children to participate in the reading by saying the repeating verses with you. At the end of the story, talk with children about how the frog gets caught and how he finally gets away.

Jumping Frogs

NCTM Standard

Patterns and Relationships

Materials

- Jumping Frogs! activity page 75
- scissors
- crayons
- tape
- paper and pencils

Ahead of Time

Copy, enlarge, and cut out six frog patterns from the activity page and let six children color them. Ask three children to color their frogs green and three to color their frogs brown. If you wish, you may copy, enlarge, and cut out seven lily pads and place them in a line on the floor.

1 This activity is a challenging cooperative game in which children use logical reasoning to reach the solution. Explain to the class that they will play a frog jumping game. Ask the six children who colored frogs to be "frogs" by taping their frog pattern to the front of their shirts. The three green frogs will then sit one behind the other on the first three "lily pads" and the three brown frogs will sit one behind the other on the last three "lily pads," with an empty "lily pad" between the green and brown frogs. The green and brown frogs should be facing one another.

One Possible Solution

5 jumps to 4

3 jumps to 5

2 jumps to 3

4 jumps to 2

6 jumps to 4

7 jumps to 6

5 jumps to 7

3 jumps to 5

1 jumps to 3

2 jumps to 1

4 jumps to 2

6 jumps to 4

5 jumps to 6

3 jumps to 5

4 jumps to 3

The goal of the game is to move by "jumps" so that the brown frogs move to the lily pads where the green frogs are sitting and the green frogs move to the brown frogs' lily pads. The brown and green frogs must work together to figure out how they are going to do this. The rules for moving:

- Only one frog from each color group can move at a time, but groups do not necessarily have to alternate taking turns.
- All frogs can move forward only (depending on the direction in which they are facing).
- Frogs can move to an empty lily pad; or a frog can "jump" over another frog to get to an empty lily pad.

Students waiting to be a frog can assist those who are acting out the problem, or you can have more than one group of six play at a time. Give all children an opportunity to be a frog.

2 Afterward, divide the class into groups and give each group of children copies of six frogs and seven lily pads. Let them color and cut out three green frogs, three brown frogs, and seven lily pads. Then have them use these paper manipulatives to try the same problem that was acted out. Challenge children to find the least number of moves to solve the problem and record their moves. Also, invite children to change the prior rules of the game. For instance, they might allow backward moves.

Across the Curriculum

🌀 **A FROG SONG** Create a class song about frogs using a familiar tune, such as "Twinkle, Twinkle, Little Star." A verse might begin: Hopping, swimming, little frog, now you're sitting on your log… and so on.

🌀 **ORIGAMI FROGS** Origami books have many patterns for making frogs. Choose a simple one and work with small groups to make origami frogs and other animals. A great resource is *Easy Origami* by Gay Merrill Gross and Tina Weintraub (Scholastic Professional Books, 1995).

Jumping Frogs!

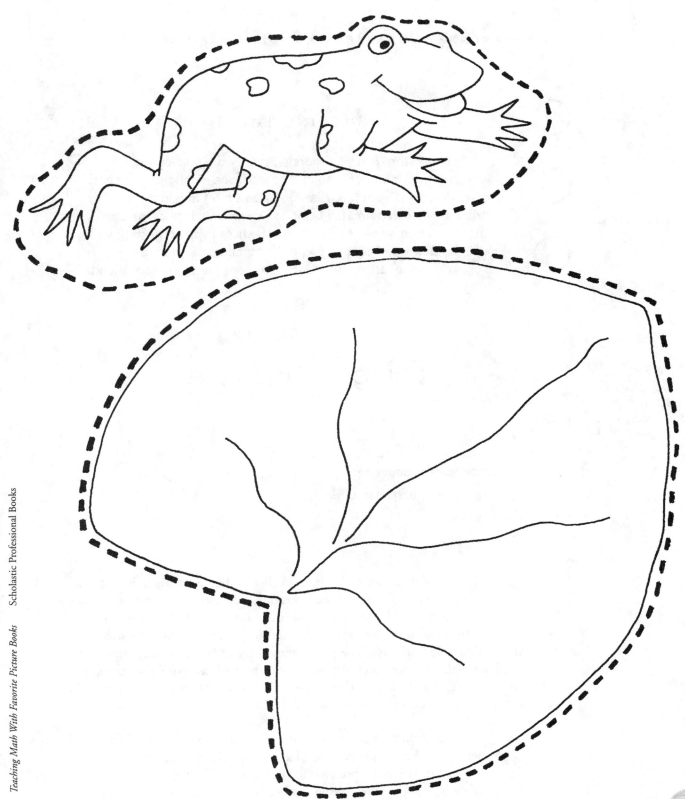

The Important Book

BY MARGARET WISE BROWN • *Harper & Row, 1949*

INTRODUCING THE BOOK

In *The Important Book*, Margaret Wise Brown discusses the important attributes of familiar objects. She highlights what each object looks like, what it is used for, and its most important attribute. Before reading the book, ask children to look at the cover illustrations and name several characteristics of each object. Have children name another object with similar characteristics, based on color, size, shape, use, or other attributes. Then read the book aloud.

NCTM Standard

Patterns and Relationships

ACTIVITY 1 Things That Are ...

Materials

- assorted old magazines
- large sheets of posterboard
- scissors
- glue stick

1 Divide the class into small groups. Distribute magazines, scissors, and glue and have each group look through magazines for pictures of objects. After each child has found two or three objects, ask the group to pool their pictures and sort them according to some common characteristics, such as shape, size, color, and use. The group should make as many categories as they need, and label a large sheet of posterboard for each category. For example, children might make a posterboard for "Things that are round," "Things that are red," and "Things you can ride in."

2 First, have children place their pictures on the posterboard. When they have settled on their categories and placement of pictures, instruct them to glue the pictures onto the posterboard and label each category appropriately. Have each group display their posters and discuss their categories with the class.

Important Things About Shapes

Materials (for each group)

🌀 construction paper shape (circle, rectangle, square, pentagon, and so on)

🌀 large sheet of posterboard

🌀 glue or paste

🌀 markers

(for the class book)

🌀 3 "O" rings   🌀 2 large sheets of posterboard

NCTM Standards

Patterns and
Relationships

Geometry and
Spatial Sense

1 Review with children various geometric figures such as circle, rectangle, square, pentagon, hexagon, and so on. Have children discuss distinguishing properties of each shape, including the number of sides and "corners," or *angles*.

2 Divide the class into groups. Give each group a different figure and have them compose a page for a class "Important Book." Children can glue their shape at the top of the posterboard and write their descriptions below. For example, the group with an octagon might write:

> The most important thing about an octagon is that it has eight sides.
> The shape of a stop sign is an octagon.
> An octagon has eight corners and its sides are the same size.
> But the most important thing about an octagon is that it has eight sides.

3 When all the groups have completed their writing, collect the pages, add a front and back cover, and use the "O" rings to assemble them into a class book that can be placed in the class library or math center.

Across the Curriculum

🌀 **IMPORTANT CLASSMATES** Have children exchange names with a partner and write a description of that classmate using the format of *The Important Book*. For example:

> The most important thing about Sara is that she is my friend.
> She has long brown hair and brown eyes.
> She is a great artist and soccer player.
> But the most important thing about Sara is that she is my friend.

You might attach a photo of the child to each description and display them on a bulletin board entitled "Very Important People in Our Class."

Jesse Bear, What Will You Wear?

By Nancy White Carlstrom

Macmillan, 1986

INTRODUCING THE BOOK

This rhyming story tells what Jesse Bear wears throughout his day. Ask children to listen carefully as you read the story. Then ask them to identify which of the things Jesse Bear wore could be placed in a set called *clothes*. On the chalkboard or a piece of chart paper make a list of these items; also list the things Jesse wore in the story that would belong in a set of things called *not clothes*.

NCTM Standards

Patterns and Relationships

Statistics and Probability

ACTIVITY

Dressing Jesse Bear

Materials

🌀 Dress Up Jesse Bear activity page 80

🌀 crayons

🌀 scissors

🌀 paper and pencils

1 Distribute copies of the activity page. Have children color each item of clothing as follows: shirts, one red and one yellow; pants, one pair blue and one pair brown; hats, one green and one purple; and then cut out Jesse and his clothes.

2 Invite children to use the cutouts of shirts and pants to figure out how many different combinations of outfits Jesse could wear. For each combination, he must wear one shirt and one pair of pants. As children make up different outfits with different combinations of the items of clothing, have them record and share their results. For example, outfits for shirts and pants would be: red shirt/brown pants; red shirt/blue pants; yellow shirt/brown pants; yellow shirt/blue pants.

3 Challenge children to add the hats into the outfit combinations, and again record the different combinations they make. Children will be surprised by how many more combinations are available when three articles of clothing are used.

Across the Curriculum

🌀 CLOTHING CLASSIFICATIONS Collect pictures of clothing that represent items worn during different seasons as well as for specific occasions. Have children take turns selecting items and telling what season(s) and/or occasion(s) each item would represent. Children can categorize clothing by season or occasion as part of the activity.

🌀 CLOTHING COMBOS With collected clothing, create a "dress-up" center in your classroom. Encourage children to explore different outfits they can create with the clothes at the center.

Dress Up Jesse Bear

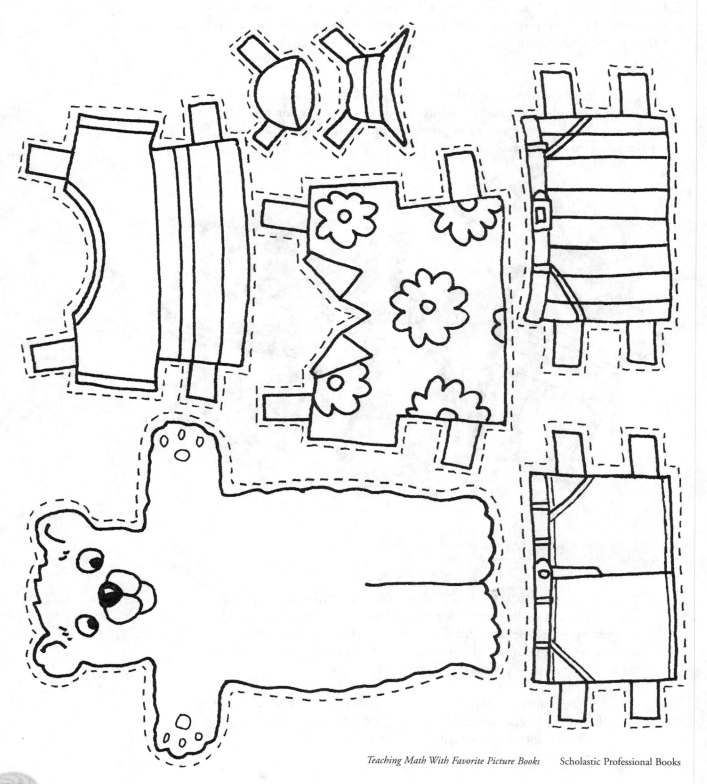